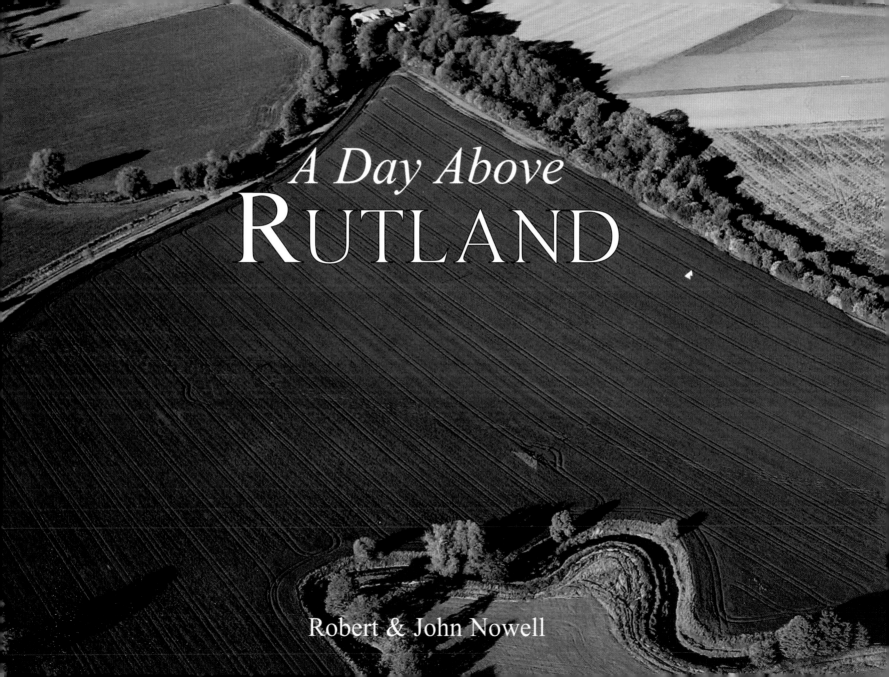

A Day Above
RUTLAND

Robert & John Nowell

Foreword

How many of us have longed as children to soar through the air looking down on our homes and gardens? It took me 60 years to realise this dream when I was taken up in nothing less than an RAF Harrier to see for myself the care taken by the Royal Air Force to minimise the inconvenience to villages and settlements when undertaking a training sortie. Needless to say, I had little time to enjoy an oversight of Rutland as all my time was taken up by the sheer exhilaration of the flight. How fortunate, then, that only a few months later this beautiful book of photographs was published enabling me to view at leisure the landscape of Rutland from the air. From the magnificence of Rutland Water to the homely layout of a village, this book brings a new perspective to our knowledge of Rutland. We are indeed fortunate to live in such a fine area and this book captures so much of what is good about our green and pleasant county.

Dr Laurence Howard,
Lord-Lieutenant of Rutland.

A Day Above
RUTLAND

John & Robert Nowell

Zodiac Publishing UK Ltd
Companies House 5330249
65 Deans Street, Oakham
Rutland LE15 6AF United Kingdom
e mail orders zodiacpublishinguk@gmail.com
www.zodiacpublishing.co.uk
1st print run   25th July 2006
2nd print run   8th September 2011
Copyright © John J. Nowell *BA FRGS LRPS*

ISBN 978-1-904566-23-6 (Padded Back).
Edited by Simone J. Nowell.
Proofing by Christine C. Nowell.
Design by William A. Nowell.
Layout by Nicholas J. Nowell.
Additional photos by Robert A. Nowell.
Scanning by Gildenburgh Media Solutions.
Printed by Toppan, Shenzhen.

Contents

Cover: A RAF BBMF Spitfire in the sunset over Rutland Water.
Title page: A heart shaped field near Belmonsthorpe.
Main title page: A vintage Auster stands ready for take off.
Inset: A RAF Harrier, two seat training aircraft. over Rutland.

Page 4/5: Oakham Castle.
Page 6/7: Oakham, showing the Castle and All Saints Church.
Page 8/9: Rutland Water glows in the early evening sunlight.
Back cover: A vintage Tiger Moth over Rutland.

Introduction by the Rt Hon Alan Duncan, MP for Rutland.

As the Member of Parliament for Rutland, and as the son of someone who saw over 30 years service in the RAF, a compendium of aerial pictures of the county is of especial interest to me. As a small rural county bang in the middle of England, one might think that Rutland would hardly figure in any study of aviation history. Not so; as so often when it comes to Rutland, there are fascinating tales to tell.

The first person to see Rutland from the air was a Mr. Sadler, the pilot of a gas-filled balloon. On the 1st November 1813, almost 200 years ago, he took off and flew 34 miles across the county. He landed at Pickworth in the midst of a hunt being led by Lord Lonsdale (pictured on horse back - top right). Whatever else Lord Lonsdale thought or said on that occasion, he would have been pleased with the colour of the balloon. The envelope was made of yellow silk (Lord Lonsdale's favourite colour) and the basket was trimmed with velvet.

The next aerial event over Rutland occurred almost 100 years later, in 1911, when the Daily Mail newspaper offered a prize of £10,000 for the winner of the 'Round England' air race. The race started at Brooklands, progressed to Hendon followed by a long straight flight to Harrogate. The route passed directly over Uppingham and Egleton and on to a field outside Melton Mowbray where the aircraft were refuelled. One aircraft landed at Egleton for repairs while another circled over Oakham before proceeding to Melton. Just five years later the war came to Rutland in the shape of a Zeppelin, which dropped bombs around Thistleton after an earlier bombing run on Nottingham. This Zeppelin was eventually shot down by Lt. W. Robinson after a two-hour aerial battle, for which he was awarded the Victoria Cross.

On the 19th June 1935, an air display was held at Green Lodge Farm, Oakham, to celebrate the jubilee year of King George V. This was the year when the expansion scheme was announced for the Royal Air Force. Advertisements appeared in the local ress seeking more young men to join the service. Only one year later it was announced, on 1st May 1936, that a new airfield was to be constructed on the plateau near Cottesmore. The airfield officially opened on the 11th March 1938 when the first squadrons, Nos. 35 and 207, arrived with their Fairey Battle aircraft. A succession of different aircraft types flew from the base including Hampdens, Skytrains and Skytroopers of the USAAF, Oxfords, Mosquitoes, Tiger Moths, Harvards, Canberras, Victors, Vulcans, Argosy, Varsity, Tornado and finally, the Harriers of No. 1, No. 3 (F) and No. IV (AC) Squadrons. Cottesmore closed as an airbase in 2011 but will re-open as a British Army barracks in the next few years. In 1939, construction started on RAF North Luffenham, adjacent to Edith Weston but in the parish of North Luffenham. It opened in December 1940 when No 17 Flying Training School, flying Tiger Moths, started operations. Ever since that time, Tiger Moths have been at home over Rutland. Bomber Command Manchesters, Stirlings and Lancasters were the next to use the air field. After WWII, the Canadians arrived with Sabre aircraft then, in 1959, it became a base for Thor missiles. Today it is home to units of the Royal Artillery.

The third airfield in Rutland, RAF Woolfox Lodge, named after the lodge that became the aircrew accommodation, opened in 1940. Manchesters, Stirlings and Lancasters operated from there during WWII. Afterwards it became the site for Bloodhound missiles which were clearly visible from the old A1. The airfield closed in 1966, the runways were then broken up and the hard core used for the repairing the A1.

On Wednesday 9th April 1941, a Junkers 88 was flying on a night intruder mission, looking for aircraft in the circuit at Cottesmore when it was shot down in flames by an aircraft from Wittering. It crash landed near the Burley to Langham road. The pilot was killed but two crewmembers baled out. One broke his leg and was 'captured' by a Mr. R. Purrot armed with a shotgun. The other crewmember, Unteroffizier Willi Lindla, lost his boots but landed safely and proceeded to walk into Oakham armed with a pistol. He passed several other people in the dark but reached Oakham without being challenged where he surrendered to the unarmed A.R.P. personnel.

War Weapons Week in May 1941 commenced with a target of £60,000. The final

amount collected was £140,314 and 12 shillings. Some of the funds went to buy the 'Stamford Spitfire' which was flown into action in September 1941 by a Rhodesian pilot. He later shot down a Messerchmitt Bf. 110 twin engined fighter.

The following year, the Rutland 'Warship Week' raised an even more impressive £191,414 fourteen shillings and sixpence, at a time when the entire population of Rutland numbered only just over 20,000. With these funds, the County of Rutland adopted H.M.S. Cottesmore; a fully-fledged naval destroyer, which earned its battle honours at D-Day and went on to serve with the Egyptian Navy as the Port Said.

During May 1943, the 'Wings For Victory' fund-raising campaign collected £225,000 two shillings and two pence which paid for five Lancaster bombers.. This magnificent effort was spurred on by some curious and sometimes startling flying operations by the newly formed 617 Squadron. On clear moonlit nights, when all other bomber squadrons were grounded, the crews of 617 hurtled over Rutland and the adjacent counties at very low level carrying out practice bombing runs down Eyebrook Reservoir. One Lancaster was reported to have clipped off the top of an oak tree near Caldecott. That branch from Rutland was removed from the tail wheel and is still visible above the bar in the former Officers Mess, now the Petwood Spa Hotel. On the night of 16/17th May 1943, nineteen aircraft of No. 617 Squadron took off and breached the Mohne and Eder dams in the Ruhr.

Today, it is possible to fly over Rutland in a variety of more peaceful ways. To drift across Rutland in a hot air balloon during the very early morning or the early evening, is an experience not to be missed. From the basket, passengers see both earth and sky from a completely different perspective. It is a gentle but thrilling experience, the sun is low the shadows long and the winds light. Apart from the necessary roar of flames, which keep the balloon aloft, it is so quiet that it is possible to talk to people on the ground as you drift overhead. As the take off and landing points vary according to the wind directions, no two flights are the ever same. By contrast, a flight around Rutland in a Tiger Moth, a wonderful two-seater biplane, is a blustery, noisy adventure. The view is magnificent and it is from this vantage point that one becomes aware of the subtle nuances of the countryside. The hidden twists and turns of rivers, roads, railway lines and even the hedgerows. The animals continue to graze since they perceive no threat. A flight over Rutland can be quite re-assuring for those of us concerned with urban sprawl and property development. From the air, the villages appear neat and small. Even the two major towns, Oakham and Uppingham, are not big despite their recent growth. Oakham and the roads around Rutland Water may have their noisy traffic problems, particularly during the summer months, but from the air the county looks very green and tranquil.

Rutland is particularly well-endowed with stone used for building material, as virtually the whole county covers a layer of Jurassic Limestone. The Oolite and Marlstone, quarried near Clipsham, has a pale brown tinge whereas the stone from Ketton is grey. Clipsham stone has been used extensively, not only for the Houses of Parliament, where I work, but also for the colleges of Oxford. From the air, the fine houses built of these local limestones are clearly visible. Burley-on-the-Hill is built mainly of Clipsham stone with a colonnade of Ketton stone. Clipsham Hall is built of stone from the local quarry. The many manor houses, lodges and cottages make a delightful and colourful contrast to the rolling agricultural countryside for which Rutland is justly famous.

A flight over Rutland will always be a memorable experience. It is such a diverse and interesting county, from its rolling hills, green fields and pretty stone villages to the sparkling waters of Eyebrook Reservoir and Rutland Water. For less than £200, one can enjoy an aerial adventure in a wicker balloon basket or the open cockpit of a vintage biplane, and see the county from the same vantage point as the early pilots did so many years ago. Until you can take to the air yourself, this book is the next best thing. It is a transport of delight, which I commend to all who will have the pleasure of reading it.

Alan Duncan,
Minister of State, Department for International Development
Member of Parliament for Rutland & Melton,
The House of Commons, London..

Chapter 1

Dawn

6 am

Even before the sun has appeared above the horizon, the balloonists have been inflating their balloons, first with cold air and then with flaming bursts of hot air. The hot air expands and the balloons 'stand up' ready for take off. The pilot completes his checks, the passengers embark and with a final burst of flame, the balloon becomes lighter than air and rises gently into the lightening sky. The passengers get their first glimpse of the crepuscular rays of the sun as it appears above the horizon - the start of another 'Day Above Rutland'.

6.15 am

In 1906, Lord Northcliffe strove to make the Daily Mail the most progressive paper in Britain by announcing a series of competitions with big money prizes. He offered £10,000 to the first person to fly from London to Manchester and £1,000 for the first person to fly across the English Channel. Louis Blériot flew across the Channel in 1909, winning the £1,000 and the newspaper a fantastic exclusive. From 1910, early aviators became frequent visitors to Rutland, often landing on the polo ground at Oakham and the high flat ground to the west of Uppingham, now the extensive playing fields of Uppingham School. Like the early aviators, the first of the balloons lifts off in the calm winds around sunrise.

6.30 am

In Barnsdale Woods, massed formations of bluebells greet the new flaring sunlight and over Rutland Water, a curving flight of Canadian geese take off in the sunrise. Long before Rutland Water was constructed, a squadron formation of RAF Fairey Battle bombers from RAF Cottesmore, were the first to take part in bombing raids at the start of WWII.

8.30 am

A youngster enjoys the fresh morning sunlight as she walks with her dog through the old Castle grounds. Oakham Castle, a Grade 1 listed building, is actually a fortified manor house and is ornamented with Romanesque architectural details, including six carvings of musicians. The Hall was used as an Assize Court until 1970 and is still occasionally used as a Coroner's Court or Crown Court and is now also licensed for wedding ceremonies. Traditionally, members of Royalty & Peers of the realm who visited or passed through the town had to pay a forfeit in the form of a horseshoe.

Other historic traditions were preserved when Normanton Church, seen silhouetted above against the morning sun, was saved from the rising levels of Rutland Water when it was dismantled and rebuilt on a promontory. It is now a museum and is now also licensed for marriage ceremonies. This page left shows an ancient apple tree framing the church of Holy Trinity at Teigh where the elegant Georgian Rectory was used by the BBC for its adaptation of Pride and Prejudice. Opposite page, top, the curious structure at Barrow is all that remains of its ancient buttercross.

7 am

A Supermarine Spitfire, illuminated from below by the morning sun, roars over Barnsdale Woods where some bluebells are still in shade. This delicate wild hyacinth creates one of the most dazzling displays (as does the Spitfire) in springtime in translucent shades of blue. Bluebells are a unique English spectacle, for only in Britain's mild, moist climate do bluebells flourish in such profusion in open, broad-leaved woodlands such as Barnsdale Woods. Opposite, the monochrome photograph

was taken only two years after Bleriot had flown the Channel in 1909. One of the first aircraft in England made an emergency landing on the Oakham polo field next to the Melton Road. At that time, such an event attracted a large crowd of curious onlookers. Today, only the vibrant sound of a Merlin engine causes a look into the sky or a view of a Spitfire model on the Oakham Bypass.

7.30 am

Before the creation of Rutland Water in 1976, there were three villages called Hambleton; Nether or Lower Hambleton (the 'lost village' now beneath the water), Middle Hambleton and Upper Hambleton. Lower Hambleton was a substantial medieval settlement and may have been the the capital of the Anglo Saxon Kings in Rutland. In 1086, the Doomsday Book recorded that the village had a population of 750, three priests, three churches, a mill and 45 ploughs at work. The imposing Jacobean Middle

Hambleton Hall, shown left, built in 1611, now stands at the water's edge, on a newly created peninsula. This Hall was once the home of Group Captain 'Johnnie' Johnson, the top scoring RAF WWII fighter ace. Left, the first fishing boat of the day gives scale to both lake and peninsula. Far left, the imposing modern Hambleton Hall was built in 1881 as a hunting box by Mr Walter Marshall of Marshalls Brewery, who came to Rutland to enjoy the fox hunting with the Cottesmore, Quorn, Belvoir or Fernie hounds. It was converted by the present owners in 1979 into the now, world-famous, Hambleton Hall Hotel.

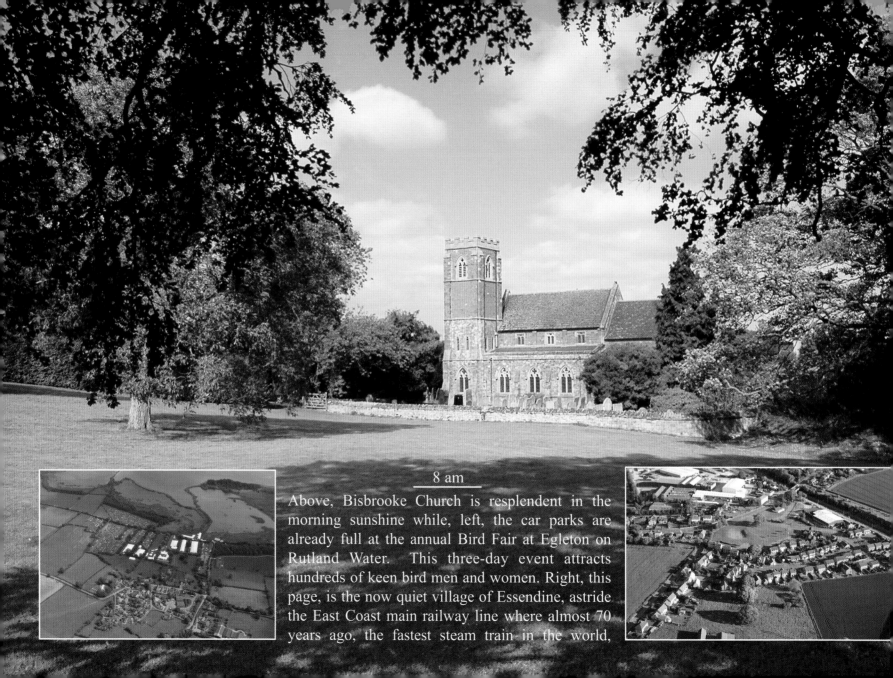

8 am

Above, Bisbrooke Church is resplendent in the morning sunshine while, left, the car parks are already full at the annual Bird Fair at Egleton on Rutland Water. This three-day event attracts hundreds of keen bird men and women. Right, this page, is the now quiet village of Essendine, astride the East Coast main railway line where almost 70 years ago, the fastest steam train in the world,

'*Mallard*' thundered through Essendine at a speed of 128.88 mph. '*Mallard*' was a LNER Pacific Class A4 4-6-2 steam locomotive designed by Sir Nigel Gresley and built in Doncaster in 1938. The A4 engines are 70 feet long, weigh 165 tons and were used to pull trains carrying 198 passengers from Kings Cross to Edinburgh, a distance of 408.65 miles - non-stop! The '*Mallard*' record still stands today. This page, the hamlet of Wardley, off the busy A47, now in a quiet cul-de-sac.

The Air Ambulance is on call every day of the year and is shown responding to the first call of the day, landing on a snow covered field in the crystal clear morning light. The sails of the nearby windmill at Whissendine are stationary in the still, calm air. The contrast between the winter scene and Whissendine in summer is dramatic, the photograph in summer being taken before the windmill regained its missing sails. Nigel Moon, the miller of Whissendine, bought the

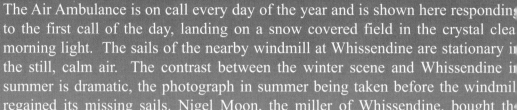

delerict mill in 1995 for £50,000. The mill was originally built in 1809 and Nigel then invested time and money to bring it back to working order. Now he runs Whissendine Windmill on his own, producing around two tonnes of flour a week. In August 2009, Nigel completed final work on the sails, to enable the windmill to work again on wind power. and demonstrates how the ancient windmill sails led aircraft and helicopter designers to adopt the same cruciform design to produce the helicopter rotor that we see today that allows the helicopter to speed to hospital at an astonishing 3 miles per minute.

7 am

From high above, an Osprey looks down on the ancient village of Edith Weston, named after Queen Edith, wife of King Edward the Confessor. Queen Edith received 'Roteland' as part of her dowry. The view of the village is in stark contrast with the ordered rows of sailing boats at the Rutland Sailing Club with space for 1,000 sailing boats and 3,000 acres of relatively sheltered water.

The Royal Forest of Rutland once covered this entire area from Braunston-in-Rutland, spreading south to Wardley, near the present A47. After the Norman Conquest, the forest became a private hunting park but at some stage, the River Chater was dammed to form these medieval fish ponds at Leigh Lodge, then deep in Leighfield Forest. By the 1600s, the demand for wood to build the new ships of King Henry VIII's Royal Navy, contributed to the entire deforestation of this landscape. The fishponds remained and are situated on a footpath that now connects Brooke Priory with Belton-in-Rutland along the aptly named 'Leighfield

Way'. Below, looking down on the village of Manton, the main railway line is hidden from view in a tunnel directly beneath the village. Once, it was possible to catch a train from Manton direct to London, one of the reasons why Asquith House, Manton was once, appropriately, home to Mr Herbert Asquith, actually a Yorkshireman from Morley near Leeds, who was Prime Minister of the United Kingdom from 1908 to 1916.

The traditional Market Place in Uppingham is the venue for many interesting events throughout the year. Left, a gathering of Classic Cars, marshalled by the Uppingham Rotary Club in support of the Derbyshire, Leicestershire & Rutland Air Ambulance Service. Shown right, seen from the Falcon Hotel, the assembly of the Cottesmore Hunt and their followers, many of whom used to depend on their livelihood on such agricultural pursuits. The Classic winner was the 1963 Austin Healey 3000A

10.30 am

The best way to see Rutland is from the back of a horse, or, possibly, elephant. Here, at the annual Boxing Day meet on Cutts Close, mounted ladies of the Cottesmore wait patiently for the off. The hunt dates from 1666 but it was Hugo Meynell, first Master of the Quorn, who virtually invented the modern practice of hunting the fox at speed in the open, and is known as the 'Father of Foxhunting'. The boundaries between the Quorn and the Cottesmore were eventually agreed by the Earl of Lonsdale. In Glaston, shown inset lower left, a circu

elephant fell down the well near Grange Farm in 1895. With great local effort, the elephant was lifted out and proceeded down the main road, presumably with an indignant trump, trump, trump, to the circus in Peterbrough.

11.00 am

The Buttercross in the market square of Oakham is almost deserted while outside Oakham Castle, Dr Laurence Howard, the Lord Lieutenant of Rutland, the personal representative of our Queen Elizabeth II, reviews troops and presents medals to those recently returned from overseas

deployments. Oakham Castle dates from the 11th century while both the Buttercross and the town pump were built in the 17th century.

11.15 am

Guests at the Barnsdale Hall Hotel and Resort, built on sloping ground leading down to Rutland Water, have superb views. Not only is it possible to see the majestic Osprey but also the occasional glimpse of the Lancaster of the Battle of Britain Memorial Flight as it passes over the distinctive

A-frame houses. Of similar vintage is the Massey Ferguson combine harvester, shown right, originally supplied under 'Lend Lease' from the USA during WWII, now lovingly maintained and still able to gather in the harvest.

WEST WITH **THE** **NIGHT**

...VA SCOTIA AFTER FLYING THE ATLANTIC

NEW YORK TIMES BESTSELLER

STRAIGHT ON TILL **MORNING**

THE LIFE OF BERYL MARKHAM

MARY S. LOVELL

11.30 am

Ashwell was the birthplace, on 26th October 1902, of a remarkable lady, Beryl Markham. She was born as Beryl Clutterbuck here in Ashwell but moved to Africa when four years old. She eventually became an aviator, horse breeder, adventuress, and aristocrat with three husbands and several lovers, including Prince Henry of England, third in line to the throne (after

King Edward VIII and King George VI). She was introduced to flying by big game hunter, Denys Finch-Hatton, (played by Robert Redford in the film 'Out Of Africa'). She made the decision to fly and in her twenties learned the skills of flying in a D.H. Gypsy Mouth from Tom Black and earned her pilot's license. She became a bush pilot and a sportswoman who logged countless hours over the African savannah and jungle. She became the first female to fly solo across the Atlantic Ocean - East to West - against the prevailing westerly wind. She departed in a single-engine Vega Gull named the 'Messenger' from London and, 20 hours later, crash-landed in Nova Scotia in September 1936. She had a successful career of her own, breeding, raising, and training racehorses and became one of the most socially prominent young women in British East Africa. In 1942, she wrote her memoirs in a book entitled, 'West With The Night'. When Ernest Hemingway read the book, he said, 'She has written so well - and marvellously well, that I was completely ashamed of myself as a writer. It really is a bloody wonderful book'. Ernest Hemingway. Beryl moved back to Kenya in 1952, becoming for a time the most successful horse trainer in the country. A film of her life entitled 'Shadow on the Sun' was made starring Stefanie Powers. Beryl Markham died in Nairobi in 1986.

11.45 am

Long before the Lancaster was even designed, the construction of Eyebrook Reservoir had begun in 1937 and was completed in 1940. The water from the dam was needed for the expanding production of steel at the huge Stewarts & Lloyds (now Corus/Tata) steelworks at Corby which had commenced production in 1933. A major contribution by Corby to the war effort was the steel pipe construction of 'PLUTO', the 'Pipe Line Under The Ocean', which carried fuel in support of the allied invasion after the D-Day landings. In 1941, the formidable Lancaster first flew and proved to be a war winner. The Lancasters of 617 Squadron practised their night, low-level flying down the Eyebrook valley to perfect their techniques. One Lancaster collected a branch of an oak tree when overshooting from

Eyebrook. The oak tree branch still hangs in the old mess, now the Petwood Hotel at Woodall Spa. On the night of 16/17 May 1943, 617 Squadron proved successful with both the Mohne and Eder dams being breached. Today, the last flying examples of both the Vulcan and the Lancaster, based with the Battle of Britain Memorial Flight, still occasionally flies down the Eyebrook Valley. The tiny village of Stoke Dry, overlooking Eyebrook, has an older and even more improbable history. It was here, in the church, that the infamous 'Gunpowder Plot' was supposed to have been hatched. However, on the evening of the 5th November 1605, guards discovered the vast store of gunpowder that would have undoubtably blown the entire Houses of Parliament to smithereens.

Chapter 3

Midday

12 NOON

The earliest datable horseshoe in Oakham Castle was presented by King Edward IV in 1470 following a tradition which has been enforced for

over 600 years. Outside the castle is the bustling market, held every Wednesday and Saturday.

<u>12.15 pm</u>

The village of North Luffenham lies south of Rutland Water and the sprawling area of North Luffenham airfield. The original Hall, was owned by the Harrington family from 1538 to 1599 and then by the Digbys until the mid-eighteenth century when it was demolished. The site of the Hall is now occupied by the popular St Mary & St John primary school seen directly above, still with a resplendent ha-ha. North Luffenham airfield was built in 1940 and was a famous bomber base in WWII and then, in 1951, was used by the Royal Canadian Air Force during the cold war. There were 3 squadrons of F-86 Sabres, 410, 439 & 441, based here and the Canadians were

very popular visitors to the County. They achieved everlasting fame when the Canadian Air Force team won the UK Tiddlywinks championship. The base was also home to Thor missiles for a time but when the cold war was won, the missiles were returned to the US. The base has now been renamed St George's Barracks and is home for units of the Royal Artillery. The former, vast, F-86 hangers have been usefully converted into an award winning, warehousing and distribution complex.

12.30 pm

Opposite, the church of St Nicholas at Pilton is almost hidden by mature elegant plane trees and nearby, shown below centre, a wall is covered with old horseshoes. Opposite, lower left, the Wheatsheaf (one of many in Rutland) sits just by the main road in Greetham while opposite, lower right, Ben the Border Terrier waits patiently for his master at the Sun Inn at Cottesmore. This page shows the village of Morcott, where St Mary's Church is of Norman origin. This quiet village is now bypassed by the busy A47.

1 pm

By 1 pm, the sun floods across Ryhall but cloud shadows obscure Belmonsthorpe above and the 11th century village of Barrowden, opposite page, where the River Welland, shown at

the bottom of the village, forms the county boundary between
Rutland and Northamptonshire

1.15 pm

The main picture shows the village of Caldecott, the most southerly village in Rutland, with Eyebrook Reservoir in the distance. Top left is the village of Egleton where the Bird Fair is held every year while lower left, a vintage tractor is laden with flowers in the village of Thistleton,

the most northerly village in Rutland. On this page, the main picture shows the elongated village of Tixover, built on a high bank above the River Welland. At the very end of the village is the isolated church of St Luke's, once, before the Black Death, in the centre of a medieval village. Inset, this page, is the village of Tinwell where a Polish para-trooper had one of the most miraculous escapes during WWII. He was the jumpmaster on a twin-engined Dakota aircraft which collided with another aircraft over Tinwell at 600 feet. As the doomed aircraft fell, the paratrooper jumped and his parachute deployed just as he landed in the mud of the River Welland, breaking both his legs - but surviving the war.

1.30 pm

The peninsula at Whitewell has more sporting and leisure activities than any other part of Rutland. Here one can swim, sail, cruise, climb, swing, paddle, jump, splash, bike, drink, eat, camp, view or simply relax with views over Rutland Water in

almost every direction. Nearby is the large village of Empingham, which is famous for the battle of Empingham which was actually fought in 1470 several miles away at a location now known as 'Bloody Oaks'. It was here that King Edward IV defeated the rebels led by Sir Robert Welles in the battle that is also know as 'The Battle of Losecoat Field. It is so-called because the fleeing rebels discarded their tunics or 'lose-coats'.

2 pm

Langham, looking east towards Rutland Water, and nearby Ranksborough Hall, built in 1893 by the very distinguished soldier, Major General Lord Ranksborough. After a 26-year army career during which he served with the Royal Horse Guards; as equerry first to Queen Victoria and Queen Alexandria then as Lord-in-Waiting to King George V. When he retired, he became the Lord-Lt of Rutland. He took his title name from Ranksborough Hill, two miles to the west of Langham. Today, Ranksborough Hall is the centre of a thriving tourism and leisure complex. Opposite, the stocks of Market Overton occupy a

peaceful location within the village. Market Overton is one of the oldest villages in Rutland and is the place where Isaac Newton grew up in the 1640s. He later went on to define the laws of gravity at Woolsthorpe Manor. In the background of the aerial view of Market Overton is the Royal Air Force base of Cottesmore which originally opened in 1938 and closed in 2009.

2.30 pm

The village of Wing overlooks Rutland Water and has one of the largest camping sites in Rutland. The only pub now in Wing is the 17th century Kings Arms dating back to 1649, a traditional, comfortable inn with accommodation. Wing Maze is hidden in the upper right of the photograph and is a medieval circular maze, actually called a *'unicursal labyrinth'*, designed for religious penitence in hat the sinner is obliged to progress, kneeling, to the centre of the maze, and back, uttering suitable prayers for forgiveness. It is still in use today! Opposite, top left shows the ultra modern water treatment plant near Wing while this page lower right is the fishing lodge where fishermen from South Africa to the Orkneys compete and then give their fish to the local DLRAA Air Ambulance. Opposite page, lower right with the big fish is the author, as a Rutland Air Ambulance volunteer, with the Anglian Water fishing wardens. On this page are the villages of Ketton, Aldgate and Geeston, once completely separate villages which have merged with modern development.

The village of South Luffenham sits astride the main A6121 from Uppingham to Stamford. In 1793, Princess Rose of the Romanies was buried at St Mary's Church and it was estimated that 20,000 Romanies attended the funeral. Opposite, the latest in a long line of CS Ellis trucks, named 'The Rutland Kite',

30

SOUTH LUFFENHAM

approaches its home base at Wireless Hill. This progressive and innovative storage and transport company is celebrating nearly 80 years of service and to this day are still proudly run by the Ellis family.

3.30 pm

The original carriageway to Clipsham Hall is flanked by a unique collection of 150 clipped yew trees, most over 200 years old. The topiary was begun in 1870 by Amos Alexander, the estate's Head Forester who lived in the gate lodge at the foot of the avenue. The clipping is now carried out each autumn by the Forestry Commission's local craftsmen. Nearby are the famous Clipsham stone quarries - the hardest of the Lincolnshire limestones. The earliest recorded use of Clipsham Stone was Windsor Castle from 1363 to 1368 and later, Kings College Cambridge in the 16th century. Above, at top, is the village of

Stretton, where the ancient crossroads of the north-south, Roman Ermine Street and the older, east-west, Sewstern Lane. The Ram Jam Inn stands on this ancient crossroads, exactly 100 miles from London where the Romans built a rest halt. This exact distance was used by Lord Lonsdale from nearby Barleythorpe, who, in 1878, entered a race to walk from Knightsbridge Barracks to the Ram Jam. He won, covering the 100 miles in 17 hours and twenty minutes. Above, the Hurricane, Lancaster and Spitfire of the Battle of Britain Memorial Flight overfly Clipsham as part of a fundraising event for the Derbyshire, Leicestershire & Rutland Air Ambulance service.

4 pm

Braunston-in-Rutland stands besides the
River Gwash and it was here, during the
restoration of the church, that a 'Celtic
Earth Mother' figure was found. It now
stands propped up against to rear wall of
the church and is possibly the ugliest
carving in Rutland. Opposite, Belton-in-

Rutland was re-named by his grace, the Duke of Rutland, to avoid confusion with other villages named Belton across Middle England. Belton means *village in the shade* and is a reflection of its ancient position within the great Royal Forest of Leighfield. Legend tells that King Charles I rested here following his defeat at Naseby and the stone base of the War Memorial is still refered to as the King's stone.

4.30 pm

Bede House, seen here in the very centre of Lyddington, was a 14th century hall, part of the medieval palace of the Bishop of Lincoln. In the early 1600s, ownership of Bede House passed to the Cecil family and Thomas Burghley founded a Jesus Hospital for twelve poor men, two women and a warden. An octaganal tower protrudes into the main street near the restored village pump and is known as the 'Bishop's Eye'. Opposite is the

hamlet of Thorpe-by-water. The 'water' is the River Welland, seen here at the very top of the picture, which forms the county boundary between Rutland and Northamptonshire and where a very determined fox crosses the shallow water.

5 pm

One wheel over the village of Ayston, near Uppingham, where the church has a curious statue of two ladies entwined. This is said to represent two one-armed girls who were born joined together but prospered as spinners amassing sufficient money to buy a field which they left to the poor of Uppingham. Further west, the long shadows fall across the church at Ridlington where isolated farms nearby are called Park Farm

and Park Lodge, reminders that Leighfield Forest was just beyond where the last stag was hunted in 1800. This page shows the village of Preston standing on one of the highest points in Rutland on the A6003 between Oakham and Uppingham.

5.15 pm

Barrel rolls across Rutland both on the ground and, top right, in the air. Left, the A1 sweeps past Great Casterton, bypassing Roman Ermine Street that eventually became the Great North Road. The remains and outlines of a minor Roman fort, named Casterton Major are clearly visible from the air in the open ground opposite the college. Beneath the soil is an extensive Roman villa awaiting excavation. It was here in the quarry at Casterton that the most complete example of a Cetiosaurus Dinosaur was found in 1968, now on display in the Leicester City Museum. Below left is the hamlet of Little Casterton, famous for its annual agricultural machinery display. Nearby is Tolthorpe Hall, an outdoor theatre where serious Shakespeare

performers present '*A Midsummer Nights Dream*'. The original medieval Hall was built in 1550 eventually becoming the home to the Rutland Open Air Theatre where the 'Stamford Shakespeare' Company staged their first production in 1977. Shakespeare himself is reputed to have performed in his play '*Titus Andronicus*' at Burley-on-the-Hill in 1596 during the New Year's Day celebrations of Sir John Harrington. At Tolthorpe, the specially constructed stage allows the King and Queen of the Fairies, Oberon and Titania, to fly down unexpectedly from the tree tops over the open air stage and into the dream sequence of the play. Lower right, the village of Tickencote, is world renowned for the unique Norman arch in the church. Over all, the restored Avro Vulcan flies across Rutland, en route from an airshow.

5.30 pm

As the Air Ambulance wings over Seaton and the Welland Viaduct, moving at a maximum speed of 168 knots - or almost 185 miles per hour or 311 kph. It will reach its destination, the NHS Trauma Centre in Kettering in just 7 minutes, preserving the golden hour of life saving. Shown opposite, is the ancient village of

Seaton, mentioned in the Domesday Book, where the George & Dragon looks over All Hallows Church, one of the longest churches in Rutland with a nave 122 feet long. The recently restored viaduct is 1,275 yards (1.166 km) long and has 82 arches, each of which has a 40 feet (12 m) span. It was completed in 1878 and is the longest masonry viaduct across a valley in Britain.

5.45 pm

In the early evening, an immaculate de Havilland DH 82 Tiger Moth, flies over Fort Henry. The Tiger Moth was designed in the 1930s by Geoffrey de Havilland and was the primary flying training aircraft of the Royal Air Force. Literally thousands of pilots were trained until it was retired from the RAF in 1952 though it is still in use by civil clubs. Note the grass trailing from the tail skid! Below, in the shadows, on the banks of the lake is the 1788 fishing folly known as Fort Henry, part

of the Exton Park Estate which has been the home of the Noel family, the Earls of Gainsborough, for almost four hundred years. The lengthening shadows stretch across the park but the main house, above, the ruins of the old mansion and the church are all illuminated. Beyond the park, down Pudding Bag Lane, two riders cross the green in the village of Exton.

Chapter 5

Evening

6 pm

At Brooke, a hamlet that has hardly changed over the centuries, the graceful curve of the shadow from the church of St Peter frames the mature graveyard. This church was featured in the 2005 film version of *Pride & Prejudice*. The source of the River Gwash is nearby and flows into Rutland Water. Opposite, the sweeping curve of the Oakham bypass encloses modern, red-roofed houses. The need for the bypass originated due to the closing of the railway crossing, which is closed for 11 minutes each hour causing traffic problems. It is noteworthy that only 60 years ago, the railway gates were always closed and only opened, on demand, when a rare vehicle approached.

6.15 pm

Above, the long rays of the sun cross the ordered layout of Wireless Hill Industrial estate with deserted car parks in the early evening. Across the valley of the River Chater, the rays of the sun also illuminate Lyndon Hall, shown right. The Hall was built around 1677 and in 1722, was the birthplace of Thomas Barker - the Father of English Meteorology. Thomas observed the weather and kept daily records from the age of 11 and faithfully maintained his observations until he died on the 29th December 1809. His 65 years of observation, including a tornado crossing Rutland, are still referred to by the weathermen of today. Beyond the rising hill is Rutland Water and the bright white hulls of the many sail boats.

6.45 pm

The graceful mansion that is Burley-on-the-Hill is itself graced by lengthening shadows as the balloons pass overhead. The present house was built in the 1690s by the 2nd Earl of Nottingham, having consulted Sir Christopher Wren. With its symmetrical wings and outbuildings forming a 'cour d'honneur', it was one of the most ambitious aristocratic ensembles of the 17th century. George Finch, 9th Earl of Winchilsea, lived at the mansion in the late 18th century and used its grounds to stage a number of cricket matches, six of them first-class, between 1790 and 1793. As late as 1814, the venue was used for a Rutland v Nottingham game. Opposite, the mellow stones of the market town of Uppingham glow in the early evening sunlight. Uppingham School was founded in 1584 by Robert Johnson, the Archdeacon of Leicester who also established Oakham School. Old boys include both Sir Malcolm Campbell and his son Sir Donald

Campbell, both holders of the world land and water speed records. The Reverend Edward Thring, who was headmaster from 1853 to 1887, is perhaps the school's best-known headmaster. His many innovative changes to the school's curriculum were later adopted in other English public and state schools. Uppingham has the greatest area of playing fields of any school in England.

7 pm

The Band of the Lifeguards
'*Beat the Retreat*' and march out
of Oakham Market Square in the
early evening sunlight.   From
above, the rays fall across the
town with Rutland Water in the
distance and causes All Saints
Church to positively glow. It is
here that the Oakham War
Memorial stands. Inset, on the
Barnsdale golf course, a player
make a final sunlit putt.

7.15 pm

A farmer in his modern combine harvestor, will continue into the night to gather in the harvest, in the path of his headlights while one of the balloons drifts high overhead. Or Rutland Water, the sailing boats head back for the shore where one of the balloons has already

landed. The pilot sits on the ground but continues to blast hot air into the
envelope to keep the balloon 'standing up', simply to help his recovery
crew to locate where he has landed

7.30 pm

'Round,
Like a circle in a spiral,
Like a wheel within a wheel,
Never ending or beginning,
On an ever spinning wheel,
Like a snowball down a mountain,
Or a carnival balloon,
Like a carousel that's turning,
Running rings around the moon,
As the images unwind,
Like the circles that you find,
In the windmills of your mind!'
Michael Legrand.

'Les Moulins de mon coeur', *'The Windmills of your mind'*, by Michael Legrand, with english lyrics by Alan & Marilyn Bergman, won the Academy Award for Best Original Song in 1968 when it was sung by Noel Harrison in the film, *The Thomas Crown Affair*. Today, these distinct shapes in the sunset easily trigger memories of the song. The sails of the 18th century, restored tower windmill at Morcott, are forever still though the bright yellow, carnival, hot air balloon sails majestically into the sunset

7.45 pm

As the sun sets, the wind drops off to virtually nil, and across the Cottesmore plateau, the balloon is almost stationary while on Rutland Water, the last of the sailing boats, also wind-dependent, drift to the shoreline.

8 pm

The swans on Rutland Water near the Hambleton Peninsula, are oblivious of the hot-ar balloon beneath the sunlit sheet of stratus cloud tracking towards Oakham. The balloon will soon make its final landing before making another flight tommorrow, for another 'Day Above Rutland'.

Many, many people were involved in making a success of this project. We would like to thank the following individuals, companies and government departments; Dr Laurence Howard, Lord-Lieutenant of Rutland who kindly wrote the foreword; Rt Hon Alan Duncan, Member of Parliament for Melton & Rutland, now re-elected for the fourth time and now Minister of State For International Development Aid - also promoting tourism into our region of Middle England and Rutland; Group Captain Andy Golledge and Wing Commander Bruce Hedley (P2 inset) who flew Dr Laurence over Rutland in the Harrier; Councillor Joyce Lucas, Mayor of Oakham - who first mentioned the phrase 'Middle England' to me; Squadron Leader Clive Rowley who was flying the Spitfire over Rutland Water when SAC Jodie Fox took the atmospheric front cover photograph; thanks to Nicola Hunt in DPA, MOD and Geoff O'Connor, Imperial War Museum (P13, 18, 23, 59 & 65) - the RAF photographs are British Crown copyright reproduced by permission of the Controller of Her Britannic Majesty's Stationary Office; thanks also to Tony Cunnane, Red Arrows and Gordon Bartley of British Aerospace. It was a pleasure to fly with the following aviators; Philip & Susan Shotbolt in the WWII vintage Auster - Phil most deservedly won the award for the best restoration project at the Air Britain Classic fly-in. He bought a 1939 Tiger Moth and restored it over the past five years. Khalid, Frank McClurg, Nick Atkinson, Patrick Bryan, Jamie Goodwin & Mike Moore at Sibson Flying School. For flights over Rutland in the vintage Tiger Moth and more modern aircraft, call 01832-280-289 or see www.nsof.co.uk; Bill & Anne Makin; John & Joanna Coleman; Cyrus Asadi; the balloonists - Alan Lusty, Ian Warrington & Peter Foot. We enjoyed the company of fellow photographers and artists; Simon Curtis (P42); Chris Lythall (P41); Yvonne Martin; Chris Hawkins, Katrina Low & Lauren Tucker (P22); Andrew Critchell (P16); Andy Miller; Paul Porter for his classic shots of the Air Ambulance (P29 & 74); Isa Asadi (P77); Ian Wilkinson for the adventurous fox (P69); Hugh Dodson (P18, 43 & 86); Simon Curtis (P42); Mikael Greinsmark (P17); Nick Neve, Oakham School (P87, 91 & 94); Ronnie Barraclough (P32); Will Cunningham (P85); Dan Smith (P22); Jamie Hunter for his photos of the Vulcan over Rutland (P44 & 73). Thanks for all the family support, especially to Simone Nowell (editing & photo P17) and Nicholas & William Nowell (who designed the book) and wife & mother, Christine, (who corrected our English). Finally, this book could not have been published without the support of Richard Tyas and Carol Bratton of First Enterprise & Mohd Ali of Peterborough Flying School and special thanks to Hayley Cook, Vickie Pauley, Sarah Plowes and Trevor Ellis, all of CS ELLIS (GROUP) LTD whose support made this production possible. In turn, it is our pleasure to support the

: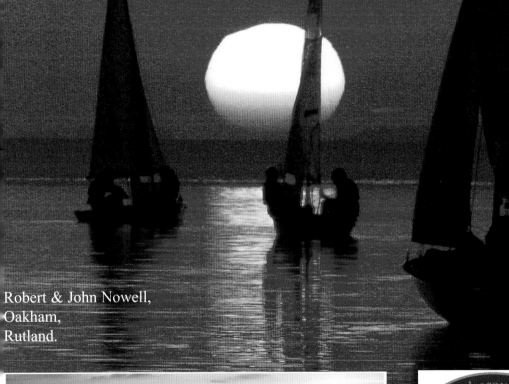

Derbyshire, Leicestershire & Rutland Air Ambulance Service including fellow volunteers and workers, Terry & Mandy Black, Sophie Stevens & Kit Chambers and the Air Ambulance Trust to build helicopter pads at major hospitals to enable 24-hour service to commence. The Air Ambulance Service relies totally on donations from the public.

Robert & John Nowell,
Oakham,
Rutland.

Ranksborough Hall
R H
Rutland

DERBYSHIRE
LEICESTERSHIRE
RUTLAND
AIR AMBULANCE

John Nowell met his wife, Christine in Changi, Singapore where she introduced him to photography. John had completed his first solo in a glider over Lincolnshire at 16. Christine Nowell was born in Skegness, the daughter of a RAF Air Gunner and grew up in Wainfleet within sight of the bombing range. John joined the Royal Air Force and flew with 206, 205 and 230 Squadrons, some of the old flying boat squadrons and it was the records of their early exploration flights that formed the basis of his 'Now & Then' series of books. His first book,

'A Day Above Oman' has been re-printed 14 times. His discovery of a collection of 5,000-year-old, perfectly preserved tombs in Om made the front page of The Times and led to a Fellowship of the Royal Geographic Society. Robert grew up in Oman and worked w John, above left, on 'A Day Above Yemen' and then, while John was working away on 'Now & Then - Bahrain', Robert and his sist Simone, produced 'Now & Then - Dubai', which has been re-printed 10 times. Incredibly, after 10 years, the book is so popular with touri that it is still in the 'Times Out' best-seller list! Robert has also produced 'Bahrain - The Grand Prix' to celebrate Formula 1 arriving Bahrain. John & Chris have lived all over the world with their six children; Marc, Kerri, Robert, Simone, Nicholas and William, three so in-law; Robert, Cyrus & Patrick; and four grandchildren; William, Isa, Max and Layla. Their next book is 'Now & Then - Qatar'.

Below are some of the other books in the series - follow us at twitter.com\zodiacbooks or visit www.zodiacpublishing.co.uk

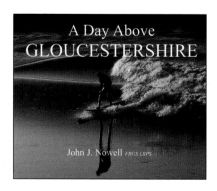

A Day Above
GLOUCESTERSHIRE

John J. Nowell FRGS LRPS

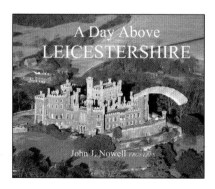

A Day Above
LEICESTERSHIRE

John J. Nowell FRGS LRPS

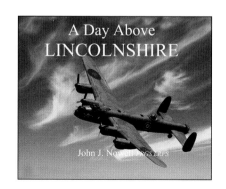

A Day Above
LINCOLNSHIRE

John J. Nowell FRGS LRPS

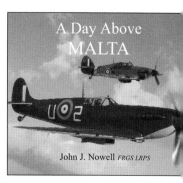

A Day Above
MALTA

John J. Nowell FRGS LRPS